The CLASSICAL mood

A Royal Occasion

A Royal Occasion

*M*any monarchs have ranked among the most important of music patrons, calling upon composers to celebrate all manner of pomp and ceremony. For George II, Handel wrote his spectacular *Music for the Royal Fireworks* and majestic *Coronation Anthem*; Haydn incorporated his hymn, *"Emperor" String Quartet* in praise of Franz II; and Elgar proudly presented his *Coronation March* to their Imperial Majesties, George and Mary. Some rulers were musicians themselves. Under the patronage of the talented Louis XIV, his court composer, Lully, became the most influential of his time. With this volume of *In Classical Mood*, you can celebrate *A Royal Occasion* in the exclusive company of sovereigns, historic and mythical, including the fairytale Tzar Saltan, the bloodthirsty Christian II, and the exotic Queen of Sheba.

THE LISTENER'S GUIDE — WHAT THE SYMBOLS MEAN

THE COMPOSERS	THE MUSIC	THE INSPIRATION	THE BACKGROUND
Their lives... their loves.. their legacies...	Explanation... analysis... interpretation...	How works of genius came to be written	People, places, and events linked to the music

---

© MCMXCVIII IMP AB   In Classical Mood™   IMP AB, produced under license by IMP Inc.   Printed in China. US P 2201 12 046

Contents

GEORGE FRIDERIC HANDEL *1685–1759*

Solomon

ARRIVAL OF THE QUEEN OF SHEBA

The Queen of Sheba is one of the most sumptuous figures in the Bible. Her kingdom was in southern Arabia, commanding the ancient sea route between the Middle East and India. According to the First Book of Kings, in the Old Testament, she visited King Solomon, builder of the great temple in Jerusalem. She arrived at the head of a camel train loaded with gifts of gold, gemstones, and rare spices. This orchestral movement celebrates her appearance in exquisite style, the infectious dancing lilt of the music swinging between strings and woodwind, while a pair of oboes provides an appropriate fanfare throughout. A harpsichord continuo keeps everybody playing in time. A modern critic commented, "If this sparkling piece really represents the Queen's arrival, then she is the merriest monarch in oratorio."

ROYAL TITLE

Handel wrote this piece as the *Sinfonia* or *Overture* for Part III of his oratorio, *Solomon*. The title, "Arrival of the Queen of Sheba," was coined by the famous conductor Sir Thomas Beecham.

SOLOMON

Handel wrote the score of *Solomon* in under five weeks in 1748. Solomon, King of Israel, lived in the 10th century BC. His great wisdom is illustrated in the story known as "The Judgement of Solomon" (*right*), in which two women claim to be the mother of the same baby. He orders the child to be cut in half and shared—knowing that the true mother would reveal herself by offering the child to the other woman rather than allow it to be harmed. The oratorio looks at the facets of royal responsibility. Solomon is shown first in his role of temple-builder and husband to a young queen, then as the wise judge. Finally, as the philosopher-king, he welcomes the Queen of Sheba, who is curious about his dazzling reputation.

HANDEL THE COLLECTOR

In 1744, Handel introduced his new oratorio, *Semele*, based on a classical myth about the love of the Roman god Jupiter for the mortal Semele. Handel owned a collection of paintings, some showing Jupiter with his paramours. These may have inspired his profane new venture, which was not a success initially.

Narcissus and Echo *by Pier Francesco Mola is believed to have been in Handel's collection.*

KEY NOTES

In later life, Handel suffered from eye problems—probably cataracts and glaucoma. Operations brought temporary relief, but by 1753 he was blind. Although this made him unhappy, he could still play his music from memory—sometimes better than ever.

JOHANN STRAUSS II *1825–1899*

Emperor Waltz

OPUS 437

Strauss's Vienna was capital of the Hapsburg Empire, the seat of a royal dynasty that looked back over 600 years of European history. By the 19th century, the Empire was in decline, but under the rule of the Emperor Franz Joseph, Vienna itself was still a glittering imperial city. Much of this comes across in this waltz, which unusually opens in march time, a sign of something special in store. A brief cello solo makes way for the main waltz tune, the most noble and dignified that Strauss ever wrote. A succession of other splendid melodies follows, confident and mellifluous, before the main theme gracefully insinuates its way back into the music. The tempo slows, the brief cello solo returns, and the grand main theme seems to be drifting away into the clouds, before a closing flourish. The whole piece is whole-heartedly symphonic in scale and feeling.

SEEKING FAVOR

Strauss wrote several pieces to celebrate the 1848 Revolution that overthrew Austria's Chancellor, Prince von Metternich. However, after his failure to succeed his father as Hofball-musikdirektor ("Director of Music for the Imperial-Royal Court Balls"), Strauss changed tack. In 1849, he wrote a march for Kaiser Franz Joseph (*left*, with his wife), marking the start of closer links with the monarchy, even as Austrian imperial power reasserted itself. He wrote a waltz for the Emperor's brother, performed for Tzar Nicholas I, dedicated waltzes to Queen Victoria and Prince Albert, and conducted at Imperial Balls in 1851.

HAND IN HAND

Franz Joseph's Jubilee in 1888 (*above*) showed all the glitter of the late Hapsburg Empire. The *Emperor Waltz* was composed a year later to fit the grandiose mood. First titled *Hand in Hand*, after a speech by Franz Joseph to Kaiser Wilhelm II of Germany about the ties between their nations, Strauss's publisher later suggested he rename his piece the *Emperor Waltz*.

KEY NOTES

Field Marshal Radetzky, who helped crush the 1848 Vienna Uprising, and with it the revolutionary leanings of Strauss II, was honored in the Radetzky March by Strauss's father.

NIKOLAI RIMSKY-KORSAKOV *1844–1908*

The Tale of Tzar Saltan

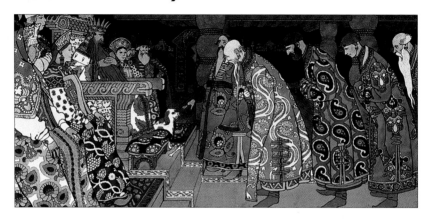

THE TZAR'S DEPARTURE AND FAREWELL

Like "Cinderella," this opera features two bad sisters who turn against the virtuous one, Militrissa. She has married the Tzar, and early in the story, her sisters conspire against her once the Tzar has left to do battle elsewhere. Here the Tzar is departing with his entourage. A brisk drum roll and trumpet call announce a lively little march, first heard on the woodwind, and given extra sparkle by cymbals and triangle. This gives way to the full orchestra, with a contrasting section from brass and strings, before the jaunty theme comes marching back.

FAIRYTALE SUITE

Rimsky made up a suite, *The Tale of Tzar Saltan— Musical Pictures*, using music from the long preludes in his opera.

WINGED LOVE

In this romantic stage drama, the Tzar's marriage to
Militrissa is ruined by the plotting of her two sisters, whom
the Tzar has passed over in his choice of a wife. Their jealousy
knows no bounds when Militrissa bears a son, Guidon, and
the sisters have mother and son thrown into the sea. They are
washed up on an island where the young prince rescues a swan
from a hawk. The swan, an enchanted princess (*below, left*) blessed
with magical powers, builds him a wonderful city (*right*). Tales
of the Prince's island reach the Tzar, but the two sisters try to
stop him from visiting it. Guidon frees
the Swan Princess from her enchantment,
marries her, and the Tzar arrives for a
joyful reunion with Militrissa.

POETIC INSPIRATION

Rimsky-Korsakov collaborated
with the librettist V. I. Belsky on creating
his magnificent four-act opera during the
winter of 1898–99. The work was based on
an 1831 poem by the Russian writer,
Alexander Pushkin (1799–1837), called
"The Tale of Tzar Saltan." The two men
tried to follow the original text as closely
as possible, planning the opera as a
centenary tribute to Russia's greatest poet. The heroine's role was
taken by Rimsky's favorite soprano, Nadezhda Zabela-Vrubel.

KEY NOTES

*The full title of
the opera includes
the main characters
from the fairy story:*
The Tale of Tzar
Saltan, of his son
the famous and
mighty hero, Prince
Guidon Saltanovich,
and of the beautiful
Swan Princess.
*It was premiered on
November 3, 1900,
at the Solodovnikov
Theater in Moscow.*

JOSEPH HAYDN *1732–1809*

String Quartet in C Major

OPUS 76 NO.3, "EMPEROR": SECOND MOVEMENT

The subject of this movement has given rise to the title of the whole quartet. Haydn initially wrote the melody as a hymn to the Austrian Emperor, Franz II: the words by Leopold Haschka began, "Gotte erhalte Franz den Kaiser" ("God Save the Emperor Franz"). It may also be familiar as the theme of the German national anthem. Played here with the purity of a classical string quartet—two violins, viola and cello—the melody conjures up the serenity of the picturesque Austrian landscape. Meanwhile, Haydn weaves some enchanting decorations and harmonies around it, in a set of four variations.

FIRST NATIONAL ANTHEM

Haydn's music for the "Emperor's Hymn" was inspired by "God Save the King" which he had heard in England two years earlier. His own anthem was first performed at the Burgtheater in Vienna on February 12, 1797, the birthday of Franz II. The audience rose to sing the hymn as the Emperor made his appearance, while at every theater in the city it was played before the evening's performance. The Emperor was so pleased with the work that he gave Haydn a golden snuff box in token of his thanks. His subjects, too, were delighted with the song and it was translated into the 14 languages recognized throughout the empire, becoming Austria's first national anthem (*below*). The *"Emperor" Quartet* was published in September of the same year.

ANNEXING THE ANTHEM

On April 9, 1946, the Austrian Federal Government invited entries for a competition to write the words to a new national anthem. The need for fresh music had arisen because the Third Reich had taken over Haydn's melody for its own anthem, so that to the world it was irrevocably associated with Hitler's Germany (*above*). The new music came from a masonic cantata, supposedly by Mozart—although this is now thought questionable. The Austrian government offered 10,000 schillings for the winning text, and received nearly 2,000 entries. The winner, declared on February 25, 1947, was the novelist, Paula von Preradovic.

KEY NOTES

A year before he composed the "Emperor's Hymn," Haydn wrote his last work for the stage: incidental music to an English play, The Patriot King, by Alexander Bicknell.

GEORGE FRIDERIC HANDEL
1685–1759

Music for the Royal Fireworks

OVERTURE

To celebrate the Treaty of Aix-la-Chapelle that ended the War of Austrian Succession in 1748, King George II planned a huge fireworks display in London on the theme of peace. He also commissioned Handel to write this Baroque suite just for the occasion. A background set featuring a triumphal arch decorated with a bas-relief of the king was erected, and a grandiose 100-instrument orchestra lavishly performed Handel's *Music for the Royal Fireworks* in front of it. The majestic French *Overture* was played before the fireworks even started. It commences with a large opening movement and then onto shorter movements. The beginning is a grand and stately flourish, with kettledrums well to the fore. Then fanfares on trumpets and horns supported by spritely strings mark the main section, during which a sturdy and energetic tune emerges. The strings slow the pace down again, before the piece proceeds to its joyous conclusion.

FIREWORKS AND FIASCO

The first performance of Handel's work had as fiery a history as the spectacle that followed. Handel (*left*) and George II (*below*) differed over the style of the music for the grand occasion. The Duke of Montague, Master General of the Ordnance, writing to Charles Frederick, "Comptroller of His Majesty's Fireworks as well as for War as for Triumph," spelled out his anxieties: "the King... objected to there being any music; but when I told him the quantity and number of martial music there was to be, he was better satisfied, and said he hoped there would be no fiddles." Handel then refused to release his score for the public rehearsal, which was cancelled several times. It finally took place on April 21, 1749 in Vauxhall Gardens, without fireworks. As 12,000 people headed for the event, London Bridge became the unpredicted scene of a Georgian traffic jam. This took three hours to clear and resulted in scuffles where several gentlemen were injured. The royal extravaganza itself took place on April 27 in London's Green Park. However, the fireworks were more effective than intended, for the staging caught fire and burnt to the ground. The French theater designer, Giovanni Servandoni, who had designed the set, became so excited by this turn of events that he grabbed a sword and accosted Charles Frederick. Fortunately, the royal company had left the scene earlier.

THE FULL WORKS

The *Overture* was played before the fireworks began. The rest of the movements in Handel's musical work for the outdoor extravaganza were: *Bourrée*, "La Paix" ("Peace"), "La Réjouissance" ("Rejoicing"), and two concluding *Minuets*.

LONG-AWAITED PEACE

The War of Austrian Succession, which broke out in 1740, was fought by Austria, England and Holland against Prussia, France, and Spain. In dispute was the right of

the Hapsburg Maria Theresa (*left*, on horseback) to succeed to the Austrian throne. George II was particularly in favor of Maria Theresa's succession, and in 1743, led troops onto the field at Dettingen in Bavaria—the last British monarch personally to lead an army in Europe. He won a resounding victory over the French, which Handel commemorated with his *"Dettingen" Te Deum*. By 1748, Europe was tired of the war and on October 7, it was brought to an end by the Treaty of Aix-la-Chapelle, confirming Maria Theresa as the legitimate ruler of Austria. As part of its terms, England retained Gibraltar and Minorca, but Maria Theresa lost Silesia to Prussia.

EARACHE

Handel was so sensitive to the tuning of instruments that the orchestra always tuned up before he arrived. One night, prior to a concert to be performed before the Prince of Wales (later King George II), someone decided to play a trick on the composer and mistuned all the instruments. When Handel gave the signal to begin, he was greeted with a discordant noise that drove him wild. Overturning a double-bass on the way, he reached for a kettledrum and threw it at the leader of the orchestra, losing his wig in the process.

KEY NOTES
The Music for the Royal Fireworks *was the last in a long line of compositions that Handel wrote for the House of Hanover.*

EDWARD ELGAR *1857–1934*

Coronation March

OPUS 65

For many, Elgar is inextricably linked with imperial pomp and ceremony. This *March*—composed for the coronation of King George V and Queen Mary, in London's Westminster Abbey on June 22, 1911—perfectly combines his two great loves of spectacle and the Empire. The composer had already distinguished himself with four of his splendid *Pomp and Circumstance Marches* (including the tune of "Land of Hope and Glory," in *No.1*), and so he knew exactly what was expected of him for such a regal occasion. Introduced by noble calls on brass and strings, the pace and mood of the piece settle appropriately into that of a solemn and majestic procession. Towards the end, the music sheds some of its solemnity and rises glowingly in the major, in what Elgar must surely have meant as a hymn of praise, not just for the new monarchs, but for the British Empire, which was then at its zenith.

CROWNED HEADS

The crown is etched into the public mind as the supreme symbol of monarchy, but it has not always been a hallmark of royalty. During the early period of the Roman empire, a turreted gold crown called the "corona muralis" was awarded to soldiers who were first to climb the walls of a besieged town or city. Coronets in the form of wreaths (*left*) were also awarded for skill in athletics, poetry, or war. The oldest royal crown is the Iron Crown of Lombardy (*right*). Said to date back 1,500 years, it was preserved in the cathedral founded in 595 by Queen Theolinda at Monza, near Milan. Legend has it that this crown incorporates the iron nails used in the crucifixion and that this is why it has never rusted.

CROWNING GLORY

William the Conqueror introduced the forerunner of more recent crowns in England. Originally a plain gold band with four ornate spikes, it was embellished by successive monarchs, until Henry IV commissioned a design that reached new heights of ornamentation. Named the Harry Crown, it was broken up by Henry V to pay for his war against France. In 1661, a new set of regalia was made for the coronation of Charles II. The total cost then was nearly $50,000 and these crown jewels are still used today. They include the famous seven-pound St. Edward's Crown (*left*), abandoned after George III's coronation, because of its weight. Reinstated by George V, it was worn by Elizabeth II for her coronation in 1953.

UNFIT FOR A KING

In May 1924, Elgar, recently appointed Master of the King's Music, wanted to compose some new pieces for the opening celebrations of the British Empire Exhibition that King George V was to attend. The King, however, put a stop to such creativity, stating that he preferred to hear "Land of Hope and Glory." This was not the only time that George V revealed limited musical taste. When asked why *La Bohème* was his favorite opera, he replied, "Because it is the shortest." On another occasion, a bandmaster arranged themes from Richard Strauss's *Elektra* for the changing of the guard at Buckingham Palace (*right*). As the music came to an end, the King sent a message over to the bandmaster: "His Majesty does not know what the band has just played, but it is never to be played again."

SECOND CORONATION

Elgar composed another work for George V in 1911. *The Crown of India*, an "Imperial masque," was to be played at the Delhi durbar (court), where he was crowned Emperor of India alongside Queen Mary (*right*), on December 12. A staggering total of 562 Indian princes turned out to welcome Their Majesties.

KEY NOTES

Another work by Elgar included at the coronation of George V was the Coronation Ode. Originally written for the crowning of King Edward VII in 1902, the Ode included—at the personal request of Edward VII—a reworking of "Land of Hope and Glory."

JEAN-BAPTISTE LULLY *1632–1687*

Le Carrousel du Roy

PRELUDE

This *Prelude* is the opening piece to one of Lully's many stage entertainments. Jean-Baptiste Lully was the leading French composer of his day and the favored musician at the court of Louis XIV, one of the greatest monarchs. During his long reign, Louis built the Palace of Versailles (*above*), where he gathered a galaxy of writers, artists, and musicians. With its resonating flourishes on trumpets, oboes, and bassoons, and tattoos on kettledrums, the *Prelude* evokes much of the ceremonial splendor of life at Versailles.

16

ROYAL FAVORITE

From humble beginnings as the son of a miller, Jean-Baptiste Lully (*right*) enjoyed a meteoric rise to fame, one of the most stunning in musical history. Born in Florence, Italy, he was baptized Giovanni Battista Lulli and at the age of 14 went to France to work as chamber boy to Louis XIV's cousin, Anne Marie Louise d'Orléans, known as "La Grande Mademoiselle." At her court at the Tuileries in Paris, Lully encountered the finest French music and, with careful instruction, revealed great talent as a guitarist, violinist, dancer, and composer. He soon attracted the attention of young Louis XIV, and on February 23, 1653 danced with the 14-year-old king in *Le Ballet de la*

nuit ("Night Ballet"). A month later he was made Royal Composer of Instrumental Music, and Louis XIV remained a friend and powerful patron throughout his career. Lully was naturalized in 1661. He held a position of immense power in the world of French music, establishing its national opera with works such as *Cadmus et Hermione* (*left*). He would rehearse performers first by singing his new opera to them, then by personally supervising their singing, dancing, and acting. Lully's impressive output included operas and ballets, together with an admirable array of motets and instrumental works. His formidable influence spread to England, the Low Countries, Italy, and Germany.

A MUSICAL MONARCH

Louis XIV (*right*) was himself a talented musician. He showed considerable musical aptitude from an early age, forming his own band of violins while still a child. He learned the lute at the age of 11, going on to study other stringed instruments, and proved extremely talented at the guitar. Louis also had a great passion for keyboard instruments, and his daily life was always punctuated by music. Every excursion or visit from an important personage was accompanied by some kind of performance. Indeed, there were more than 150 official musicians at the royal court and Louis insisted that all his palaces had their own theaters and music rooms. In 1669, he founded the Académie de Musique.

STABBED IN THE FOOT

Lully's extraordinary life came to a close in a particularly ironic way. Louis XIV was faced with the ordeal of intestinal surgery. Although many feared the outcome, Lully (*left*) had more confidence in the king's surgeons and composed a "Te Deum" in anticipation of his patron's recovery. The king survived and Lully's piece was performed on January 8, 1687. While conducting the work, Lully hit his foot instead of the floor with the long pole which he used to beat time. The injured toe became septic, then gangrenous. Unlike the king, he was not blessed with recovery, and died on March 22, at the age of 55.

KEY NOTES

Lully had a fearsome temper. If a violinist offended him during rehearsals, it was not uncommon for him to seize the instrument and break it over the performer's head.

JOHANN SEBASTIAN BACH *1685–1750*

Brandenburg Concerto No.3

BWV1048: FIRST MOVEMENT

Bach worked for or met a variety of royal personages in his time. One of these was Christian Ludwig, Margrave of Brandenburg, to whom the composer dedicated a set of six concertos. *Brandenburg Concerto No.3* is scored for a small group of strings, plus the standard harpsichord continuo, or accompaniment. This movement is bright and spacious in sound, and beautifully in keeping with the ambience of a handsome Baroque palace. Although there are solo passages, generally the music is closer in style to that of a Baroque concerto grosso, written for a group of instruments as a whole, rather than in the style of the later Classical concerto, with an extended part for solo instrument.

MISSING

This movement is not followed by the usual slow, second movement, although Bach may have improvised one on harpsichord. Today, a slow movement from another Bach work is often played.

KEY NOTES

It seems that Christian Ludwig, the dedicatee of the concertos, did not actually have the financial means to finance an orchestra for their performance.

JEAN SIBELIUS *1865–1957*

King Christian II *Suite*

OPUS 27: SERENADE

Sibelius's *Suite* was his first orchestral music to be published by the important Berlin publisher, Breitkopf & Härtel. He prepared it by rearranging his incidental music for a play, based on the life of Christian II, king of Scandinavia. This "Serenade" is the third of the *Suite*'s four movements, and originally introduced the final act of the play, which opens with a scene of celebration at court. It recalls one of the more peaceful episodes in Christian's tempestuous life. The rhythm of a minuet suggests a courtly dance, while horn and trumpet calls add a fitting touch of pageantry. The piece ends with the softest of scales on flutes, like a breath of sweet night air.

SMALL SCORE

Sibelius scored his orchestral suite for a small orchestra, partly because Finland was short on musicians. For example, he noted that he could find only two bassoon players, one of whom was suffering from consumption. Probably because of this, the composer said that the on-stage serenade, "Musette"—intended for two clarinets and two bassoons—"should be for bagpipes and reeds."

TROUBLED HISTORY

Scandinavia was made up of many small kingdoms until the Union of Kalmar in 1397 joined Norway and Sweden to Denmark, to form the second largest collection of territories in Europe. Their ruler was Queen Margaret of Denmark, who had her great-nephew and heir, Duke Erik VII of Pomerania, crowned King of Norway, Denmark, and Sweden at Kalmar. A century later, the monarchy contributed to one of the bloodiest periods of north European history. Christian II (1481–1559) (*right*) took action against Sweden, which had been rebelling against the Kalmar Union for 70 years. He waged a vicious three-year war against the Swedish regent, Sven Sture, and on his victory executed more than 80 of Sture's followers (*above*).

STAGE MUSIC

In 1898, Sibelius wrote music to accompany the play *Kuningas Kristian II* ("King Christian II") by his great friend, the pianist and playwright, Adolph Paul. The story, based on historical events from the reign of King Christian II, tells how the monarch falls for a low-born Dutch girl, Dyveke, who is finally poisoned. Though very popular at the time, Paul's work has now disappeared from circulation and it is mainly through Sibelius's score that the story survives.

KEY NOTES

Sibelius once told a pupil: "Never pay attention to what critics say. Remember, a statue has never been set up in honor of a critic!"

LUDWIG VAN BEETHOVEN *1770–1827*

Piano Concerto No.5

OPUS 73 "EMPEROR": THIRD MOVEMENT

Beethoven's last piano concerto is sometimes simply referred to as "Emperor," giving rise to the idea that it was inspired by Napoleon, whom Beethoven once admired. In fact, the name simply denotes the majestic, triumphant character of the music. Here, in the finale, the solo piano plunges straight in with a robust theme soon joyously embellished by the orchestra. A second theme, deceptively simple at first, leads to a profusion of new ideas. These are worked out in a flowing, expansive middle section, including a return of the opening theme. The pace then slows, as the music fades away on hushed piano chords and muffled drum beats, before a final flurry of keyboard runs and one last orchestral statement of the main theme.

COMPOSING UNDER FIRE

Beethoven wrote this concerto in 1809—a turbulent time, when the French under Napoleon were poised to invade Vienna. On May 4, his most important patron, Archduke Rudolph of Austria, fled with his family from the capital. The French began their onslaught a week later (*below*), and Beethoven retreated to his cellar as shells flew overhead. Within hours the city surrendered but everyday life was shattered, and many people were forced to beg on the streets. Beethoven wrote to a friend: "What a destructive, disorderly life I see and hear around me, nothing but drums, cannons and human misery in every form."

MIXED RECEPTION

The "Emperor" was not premiered until November 28, 1811. By this time, Beethoven was too deaf to perform as the soloist, as he had planned. However, the work went over well with the Leipzig audience who had long awaited the performance. Friedrich Schneider (*right*) played the solo part, and his mastery of the piece, together with the skill of the Gewandhaus Orchestra and the conductor Johann Schulz, combined to make the evening a tremendous success. This was not the story at the Viennese premiere three months later. On this occasion, Beethoven's innovative music prompted a much colder reception and the criticism that he was too proud and confident!

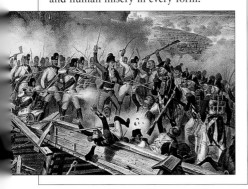

KEY NOTES

When the Piano Concerto No.5 was finally published in 1811, Beethoven found so many mistakes in the printed score that he was outraged. He berated the publishers Breitkopf & Härtel, "Mistakes, mistakes! You are a great mistake yourself!"

GEORGE FRIDERIC HANDEL *1685–1759*

Coronation Anthem No.4

ZADOK THE PRIEST

he coronation of George II was an ideal occasion for Handel to display his sublime gift for choral writing. This anthem, inspired by the biblical figure of Zadok the Priest, who anointed Solomon as king, has since remained part of the coronation ceremony in Britain since 1727. It opens in hushed and expectant mood, with a series of pulsing chords on woodwind and strings. This makes the sudden entry of the chorus all the more electrifying. "'Zadok the Priest!" they exclaim. Then comes a change of tempo, marked by trumpet calls. Sections of the chorus pass the joyful phrases back and forth with fervor—"Rejoice! God Save the King! Long Live the King! May the King Live Forever! Hallelujah!" Finally, the organ rises up with orchestra and chorus in a resounding conclusion.

SOLEMN MOMENT

Shortly before his death, George I signed "an Act for naturalizing George Frideric Handel and others." Handel's first royal commission as a naturalized British citizen was to write the music for George II's coronation. He finished it in just over a month (original score, *left*) and the ceremony took place on October 11, 1727 in Westminster Abbey, London. Sung during the Anointment of the King, "Zadok the Priest" was one of four anthems Handel wrote for the service. The other three, based on a number of Psalms, are "The King shall Rejoice" (Crowning), "My Heart is Inditing" (Coronation of the Queen) and "Let thy Hand be Strengthened" (Recognition).

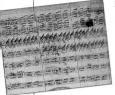

FAITHFUL SERVANT

The dying King David (*below*) appointed his son, Solomon, (seen with his mother, Bathsheba) heir to the throne of Israel. Adonijah, Solomon's elder brother, had tried to usurp the throne, but Zadok the priest and Nathan the prophet had no part in this. David ordered that Solomon be anointed king by Zadok and Nathan. Solomon was joyfully received in Jerusalem, and he rewarded Zadok for his fidelity by making him High Priest.

KEY NOTES

Handel's four Coronation Anthems were sung by a choir of 47 male voices taken mainly from the Chapel Royal, together with several operatic performers and an orchestra of 160 players, "besides an Organ, which was erected behind the Altar."

Credits & Acknowledgments

PICTURE CREDITS

Cover /Title and Contents Pages/ IBC:
Rex Features
AKG London: 5(t), (Ivan Bilibin: The Tale of Tsar
Saltan) 6, 9(l & r), 14(r), (Pierre Patel: Versailles)16,
(Jan Onghers: Musical Session Round the Table) 19,
(Lucas Cranach: Portrait of Christian II) 21(b),
Erich Lessing 14(tl); Ashmolean Museum, Oxford:
3(bl); Bridgeman Art Library, London/Private
Collection 2, 18(t), 25(r), York City Art Gallery
(Dutch School: The Judgement of Solomon) 3(r),
Historisches Museum der Stadt, Vienna 5(b),
Tretyakov Gallery, Moscow (Mihail Alexsandrovich
Vroubel: The Swan Princess 7(l), British Library,
London 10, 12(r), 25(tl), Private

Collection (Thomas Hudson: Portrait of George
Frederick Handel) 11(l), Coram Foundation, London
(John Shackleton: Portrait of George II) 11(r),
Schloss Schonbrunn, Vienna (Martin Mytens II: A
Cavalcade in the Winter Riding School, Vienna)
12(l), Giraudon/Musée Condé, Chantilly (Pierre
Mignard: Lully) 17(r); Britstock-IFA: 4, G.
Gräfenhain 8; E.T. Archive: 20, 23(l); Mary Evans
Picture Library: 18(b); Getty Images: 15(t), 22;
Hulton Getty: 13, 15(b), 24, 25(bl); Lebrecht
Collection: 7(r), 17(l), 23(r); M-Press Picture
Library: 21(t); Rex Features: 14(bl).

All illustrations and symbols: John See